MUSTARDS, KETCHUPS & VINEGARS

DIPS & DRESSINGS, SAUCES & OILS

MUSTARDS, KETCHUPS & VINEGARS

DIPS & DRESSINGS, SAUCES & OILS

Carol W. Costenbader

A Storey Publishing Book

Storey Communications, Inc.
Schoolhouse Road
Pownal, Vermont 05261

*The mission of Storey Communications is to serve our customers
by publishing practical information that encourages personal
independence in harmony with the environment.*

United States edition published in 1996 by
Storey Communications, Inc.
Schoolhouse Road, Pownal, Vermont 05261

Produced by Weldon Russell Pty Ltd
43 Victoria Street
McMahons Point, NSW 2060, Australia

A member of the Weldon Owen Group of Companies

© Weldon Russell Pty Ltd 1996

Chief Executive: Elaine Russell
Publisher: Karen Hammial
Managing Editor: Ariana Klepac
Project Co-ordinator: Megan Johnston
Editors: Libby Frederico, Kayte Nunn
Editorial Assistants: Elizabeth Connolly, Cassandra Sheridan
Designer: Honor Morton
Illustrator: James Gordon
Food Stylists: Penny Farrell, Kay Francis
Photographers: John Callanan, John Hollingshead
Production: Dianne Leddy

Special thanks to Lynda Spivey, CHE, Home Economics Extension
Agent, North Carolina Cooperative Extension Service.

Produced by Mandarin Offset, Hong Kong
Printed in China

Library of Congress Cataloging-in-Publication Data
Costenbader, Carol W.
    Mustards, ketchups & vinegars: making the most of seasonal
    abundance/Carol W. Costenbader.
        p.   cm. — (The well-stocked pantry)
    Includes biographical references and index.
    ISBN 0-88266-813-7 (hardcover)
    1. Condiments. I. Title. II. Series.
    TX819.C56 1996
    641.6'382—dc20   95–42378
                                CIP

Contents

INTRODUCING THE BASICS

*B*eyond mayonnaise, Tabasco, and yellow mustard, there's a whole world of unique flavors and grainy textures just waiting to be discovered. Condiments are used to their best advantage when they both embellish other foods and complement their flavors.

Many condiments were first introduced as healers and medicines. Evidence of oils and vinegars being used as soothing balms for the ill effects of the desert sun or as antiseptics has been found to date from the time of Christ. What reader doesn't know a granny who made a cough potion of honey and bourbon, later in the day diluting it and using it as a "refresher"?

The ancient Egyptians chewed mustard seed with their meat dishes to give flavor and to mask the meat's rancid taste. The Greeks, East Indians, and Romans are also said to have used the leaves and seeds of the mustard plant as early as 3000 BC. Everyday food was frequently spoiled due to lack of suitable storage facilities, and the strong flavor of mustard seeds hid the evidence. Vinegar is thought to have been a condiment that was used at around the same time.

Today, mustards and other condiments embellish and "dress up" the entire meal. As simple as ketchup on a hamburger or as complex as an expensive crock of imported mustard, condiments add that piquant flavor that doesn't alter the taste, but rather enhances or complements it.

This book is meant to get you started on an endless creative road of possibilities, using contemporary preserving techniques and recipes that have never appeared in print before. All recipes have been fully tested and will provide the inspiration for you to go on and create your own taste sensations. Try pineapple juice as a substitute for vinegar, or mix spicy mustard with marmalade for a sauce to accompany roasted pork or lamb. You're limited only by your imagination!

GETTING STARTED

As always, choose the freshest ingredients, and work quickly after harvest. Fruit should be mature for highest sugar content. Unlike fruit, vegetables should be young and tender. Herbs also should be picked early in the day before the sun begins to wilt them. If buying your produce you may want to carry a cooler to the market to bring it home at its very freshest. All produce should be clean, dry, and free of bruises. Keep all work surfaces, dish towels, equipment, and especially your hands, as clean as possible. Wash all containers well and fill with boiling water, using a funnel. Leave the water for 10 minutes; then pour it out and turn the containers upside down on clean dish towels.

The recipes in this book generally call for storage of 2 days–4 weeks in the refrigerator. However, when in doubt, contact your local authority. Never change a recipe's storing instructions without first consulting a professional.

Sometimes it is best to first steep vinegars and flavorings in a wide-mouthed, clean jar and remove the herbs or spices from the liquid before bottling in a more decorative narrow-necked bottle. This is a judgment call. Frequently, as in the case of garlic cloves, some spices and herbs continue to impart their flavor long after other herbs and spices are finished. On the other hand, fresh herbs, lemon peel, or cranberries can be quite pretty suspended in clear, sparkling, amber vinegar.

Salt, alcohol, vinegar, and oil are natural preservatives when used in large amounts. In ancient times, these were used to extend the freshness of everything from herbs and fruits to meats. After "soured wine" was discovered to be useful, probably by accident, vinegars became in great demand for preserving and flavoring foods. Concoctions made with various oils and alcohol appear frequently in early cookbooks and were used for medicinal and restorative purposes as well as preserving. For centuries, the fishermen of the Iberian peninsula (and, indeed, all around the entire Mediterranean seaboard) dried and salted their summer catch; these fish were winter staples and today are the basis of many national dishes.

Most ingredients can be found in a good health food store. However, there is a list of mail-order sources at the end of this book you can contact if you are unable to get hold of everything locally.

SPICES

Never use last year's half-filled spice can for this season's tastiest results. Whole, pungent, new spices are preferred. Ground spices can cloud and detract from the finished product. Remember to remove spices when canning (bottling) is through if the recipe dictates this. Spices left in an infusion may continue to add color and impart strong flavor, thereby drastically changing the taste and appearance.

OILS

Tasting oils is like sampling wines. From the fruity golden-yellow of olive oil to the pale white neutral of safflower to the richness of pungent oils infused with hazelnuts or walnuts, the possibilities are endless. Oils are basically used to carry the flavoring of salad dressing, pickles, or whatever the recipe specifies. You'll want to try many different ones until you discover the range of flavors that suit you best. Always store oils in a cool place. Try to buy cold-pressed oils because the flavor is better than oils that are treated by solvent extraction. After 6 months, oils can become rancid. Always check first by tasting a small amount before using in recipes.

OLIVE OIL The olives are pressed three or more times. The first pressing is extra virgin and is the most pure and expensive. Stone presses draw the rich, greenish oil from choice olives. The second time the same olives are heated and higher pressure is used. Various names for this are fine olive oil, superfine olive oil, and virgin olive oil. This is slightly more acidic than extra virgin. Pure olive oil is from a third pressing and can contain presses from other second and third pressed olives and/or lower quality olives. Sometimes higher grade oil is added to improve the flavor.

SESAME OIL Made from sesame seeds, it is usually combined in cooking with other oils, because the flavor is quite strong. It is used often in Chinese cooking.

GROUNDNUT (PEANUT) OIL This has a very distinct groundnut flavor when cold pressed, and a high point of smoking. It is frequently used in Chinese cooking as well.

OTHER NUT OILS Almond and hazelnut oils are made by crushing the nuts, heating them, and then pressing the paste by machine until all the oil is extracted. Almond and hazelnut oils are light and subtle; walnut oil has a more pronounced flavor. Walnut-oil processing calls for dried nuts that are then cold pressed. European in origin, these oils add a delicate flavor to salad dressings, fresh vegetables, and dips, to name a few.

PLAIN VEGETABLE, SAFFLOWER, OR CORN OILS These are generally not recommended for preserving. Their flavor is lacking and is better used for sautéeing when no taste should be imparted.

VINEGARS

Vinegars are really fermented fruit juices or grains. They vary greatly in taste and acidity. Avoid all metal containers other than stainless steel when using vinegar for preserving because other metals are reactive to the acid content of the vinegar. Make certain you use clean stainless steel pots, glass jars and bottles, or ceramic crocks. Use white vinegars when the brown or red kind would spoil the outcome (in color). Always avoid using raw or·non-distilled vinegar, as it is unstable. Also, always avoid boiling for 30 minutes or longer, as this can change the acidity of the vinegar solution. Making your own vinegar with wine and water is beyond the scope of this book and defeats the author's purpose of offering easy, creative, and unique recipes. While making your own vinegar is relatively easy, it requires special equipment and resources for the "mother" solution needed for the finished product.

Aged vinegars are preferred to the common supermarket varieties. Labels will indicate if the vinegar inside has been aged. The amount of acidity will also be printed on the label. Six percent and slightly above is ideal for our purposes here. Once you discover the difference between the aged varieties and the lifeless, pale supermarket kind, you'll be destined to choose the aged forever.

RED WINE VINEGAR This is mild and very popular. It is made from red-grape wine.

WHITE WINE VINEGAR White wine vinegar is really off-white in color and has a very delicate taste, like the white wine from which it has been made.

CHAMPAGNE VINEGAR This is authentically made only in France from wine produced in the Champagne district.

SHERRY WINE VINEGAR This is darker and stronger than the other wine vinegars, with a definite flavor of sherry. Imported from Spain, it is rather expensive.

APPLE CIDER VINEGAR Apple cider vinegar is aged from pure apple cider. It is mellow and rich in flavor.

RICE VINEGAR Rice vinegars are fermented from red and white rice wines. The Japanese varieties are very subtle and delicate, while the Chinese types are sweet and sour, and frequently contain sugar.

MALT VINEGAR Malt vinegar is dark and very popular in England and Canada. It is fermented from beer. It is used most effectively in potato salad, pickles, and with cold roast beef and other pungent foods.

BALSAMIC VINEGAR Balsamic vinegar, made only in Italy, is dark reddish brown in color and very fragrant. Fermented and aged from white grape pulp or pomace, authentic balsamic vinegar must be made in the Emilia Romagna region near Modena. It is highly regarded worldwide and is a favorite for salads, marinades, as a meat-sauce ingredient, and is even enjoyed as a flavoring for club soda!

WHITE DISTILLED VINEGAR White distilled vinegars are used primarily in the manufacture of pickles and relishes. Their clear and colorless properties make them perfect for pickling most vegetables.

SALT

Salt is used for flavoring in canned foods, but it can be a preservative agent in high quantities. Cooking and canning salt is in a pure state. Table salt usually contains iodine or agents to prevent caking. Canning salt has the same density for measuring as table salt.

Brine solution is simply canning salt dissolved in the proper volume of liquid. The percentage of brine can allow proper fermentation or, if high, can actually control the growth of salt-tolerant bacteria. Recipes in this book will clearly explain how much salt and liquid to combine to acquire the proper brine percentage.

RECOMMENDED SUGAR AND SWEETENERS

Generally use granulated table sugar, beet, or cane sugar unless otherwise instructed. The sugar in jams and jellies helps the mixture to gel and enhances the flavor. In larger quantities sugar acts as a preservative. One teaspoon has 18 calories (74 kilojoules).

LIGHT CORN SYRUP Light corn syrup enhances the gloss qualities of jams and jellies. Substitute 25 percent of the sugar called for in a recipe with light corn syrup. One teaspoon has 20 calories (82 kilojoules). Light corn syrup is also called glucose.

HONEY Light, mild honey can be used up to 50 percent as a replacement for sugar quantities. It has double the sweetening power of white table sugar. Recipes will have to be cooked for 8–10 minutes longer, but not more than 20 minutes, depending on whether the recipe uses pectin or is a cook-down variety. Recipes made with honey instead of sugar will be a bit thicker in texture. Honey is approximately 60 percent fructose and 40 percent glucose.

ASPARTAME This artificial non-nutritive sweetener can be used in some recipes to equal the amount of sugar called for. Be certain to add it last, after mixing. This product can only be used in uncooked freezer fruit recipes. It is not recommended for canned or cooked fruit.

FRUIT AND VEGETABLE KETCHUPS

*F*rom the spicy fish sauces of Malaysia to the seasoned purées of China, ketchups have been used throughout most of the world since the seventeenth century. Today, we usually think of ketchups as being seasoned tomato purées, but occasionally they may have as their primary ingredient mushrooms, walnuts, jalapeño chilies, soy beans, or even a fish base.

No wonder ketchups are so popular, their rich flavors enhance everything from hamburgers to scrambled eggs to fish and chips. Although they may take on slightly different forms in various parts of the world, ketchups are enjoyed throughout North America, Australia, in parts of the Orient, and in most parts of Europe. Commercial ketchups have usually had a great deal of salt and sugar and possibly preservatives added and are to be avoided if at all possible.

For the ideal tomato ketchup of today, set aside a late summer morning when the harvest is rolling with inexpensive, beautifully ripe tomatoes for making some of the delicious recipes in this book. Your time will have been well spent when you taste the finished product, and you will have ample supplies of flavorsome sauce to enhance your winter menus.

HOMEMADE TOMATO KETCHUP

You'll like this recipe for its blended flavors, and for not having to peel the tomatoes!

Equipment

large stainless steel saucepan
ladle
strainer
large mixing bowl
mixing spoon
funnel
storage bottles
labels

Ingredients

10 lb (5 kg) ripe tomatoes

1 large red (Spanish) onion

1 cup (8 fl oz / 250 ml)
apple cider vinegar

1 cup (6 oz / 185 g) packed
brown sugar

2 tablespoons salt

1 teaspoon cayenne pepper

1 teaspoon ground cinnamon

1 teaspoon ground allspice

1/4 teaspoon grated nutmeg

1 teaspoon baking soda
(bicarbonate of soda)

Finished Quantity
1–1 1/2 quarts (1–1.5 l)

1 CHOP TOMATOES AND ONION AND COMBINE Finely chop the tomatoes and onion. In a saucepan, cook them over a moderate heat for 30 minutes or until soft.

2 STRAIN Remove from the heat and force the tomato mixture through a strainer. Include as much pulp as possible. The mixture will be thin.

3 RETURN TO HEAT, ADD REMAINING INGREDIENTS AND SIMMER Pour the strained tomato mixture back into the saucepan and reheat. Stir in the vinegar, sugar, salt, spices, and baking soda. Simmer for 1 1/2–2 hours until thick, stirring occasionally.

4 BOTTLE Ladle the ketchup, through a funnel, into sterilized bottles (see page 18), label, and refrigerate for up to 1 month. Double this recipe and process in a boiling water-bath canner (see page 41), leaving 1/4 inch (0.5 cm) headspace, for 20 minutes for longer-term storage.

PERFECT TOMATO KETCHUP

This recipe will perfume your house with its pungent aroma.

Equipment

storage jars
sharp knife
chopping board
large stainless steel saucepan
mixing spoon
ladle
strainer
cheesecloth (muslin)
string
funnel
labels

Ingredients

10 lb (5 kg) ripe tomatoes

2 medium yellow onions

1 cup (8 fl oz / 250 ml) apple cider vinegar

1 cup (6 oz / 185 g) packed brown sugar

2 tablespoons salt

1 teaspoon cayenne pepper

1 teaspoon baking soda (bicarbonate of soda)

2 cinnamon sticks

2 teaspoons whole allspice

Finished Quantity
1 1/2 quarts (1.5 l)

1 STERILIZE JARS Check the jars for cracks or chips, discarding any that may be damaged. Also check the closures between the jars and lids, insuring that there is no seepage. Fill the jars with boiling water. Let stand for 10 minutes. Pour off the water and turn the jars upside down on clean dish towels to dry.

2 PREPARE TOMATOES AND ONIONS Finely chop the tomatoes and onions and place them in a saucepan.

3 COOK Simmer the tomatoes and onions over low heat for about 30 minutes, or until soft.

PREPARATION TIPS

❧ Start with clean equipment, dish towels, and especially hands. Choose mature fruit that is clean and free from bruises.

❧ 1/4 teaspoon grated nutmeg can be added for extra flavor.

4 STRAIN Remove the pan from the heat and press the tomato and onion mixture through a strainer to make a pulp. The mixture will be very thin.

5 RETURN TO PAN AND ADD VINEGAR AND SEASONINGS Return to the saucepan and stir the vinegar, sugar, salt, cayenne pepper, and baking soda into the tomato mixture.

6 MAKE SPICE BAG AND ADD Place the cinnamon sticks and allspice in the cheesecloth, tie with string, and float it in the tomato mixture. Simmer, uncovered, over medium heat for about 2 hours, stirring occasionally and being careful not to let the mixture burn. After 2 hours, remove the spice bag.

7 BOTTLE Ladle the ketchup, through a funnel, into the sterilized jars.

8 SEAL AND STORE Covér, label, and store in the refrigerator. This recipe will keep for 2–3 months and can be doubled easily.

MOTHER'S KETCHUP

Easy pre-cooking preparation makes this a favorite recipe.

Equipment

food processor
stainless steel saucepan
cheesecloth (muslin)
string
tongs
ladle
funnel
storage bottle
label

Ingredients

5 lb (2.5 kg) ripe tomatoes

1/2 onion

1 stick celery

1 clove garlic

1/2 bay leaf

1/8 teaspoon celery seeds

1 small dried red chili

3/4 teaspoon mustard seeds

1 cup (8 fl oz / 250 ml) champagne vinegar

4 teaspoons honey

2 teaspoons molasses

Finished Quantity
2 cups (16 fl oz / 500 ml)

1 **PURÉE TOMATOES** Quarter the tomatoes. In a food processor, process the tomatoes until smooth, about 1 minute, then remove and set aside.

2 **PURÉE ONION, CELERY, AND GARLIC** Process the onion, celery, and garlic in the food processor, adding about 1/4 cup (2 fl oz / 60 ml) of the tomato mixture to facilitate puréeing.

3 **COMBINE TOMATOES AND ONION MIXTURE** In a saucepan, combine the tomatoes with the onion mixture. Stir over medium heat for 5 minutes.

4 **MAKE BOUQUET GARNI AND ADD TO MIXTURE** Place the bay leaf, celery seeds, chili, and mustard seeds on a cheesecloth square, gather up all 4 corners, twist together, and tie with string. Drop the bouquet garni into the tomato and onion mixture.

5 **ADD REMAINING INGREDIENTS** Stir the vinegar, honey, and molasses into the tomato and onion mixture and cook for 30 minutes.

6 **REMOVE BOUQUET GARNI AND STRAIN** Use a pair of tongs to remove the bouquet garni, discard. Cook the tomato mixture for a further 10 minutes until

thickened slightly. Stir occasionally, being careful not to let the mixture burn. To remove any seeds, press the mixture through a strainer or food mill, if desired.

7 **BOTTLE, SEAL, AND STORE** Ladle, through a funnel, into a sterilized jar (see page 18). Cap tightly, label if desired, and refrigerate the ketchup for up to 2 weeks.

SHOPPING TIPS

☙ *If you are unable to find champagne vinegar in your area, you can substitute white wine vinegar instead.*
☙ *Celery is available year-round. Choose firm bunches that are tightly formed, with leaves that are green and crisp.*

CRANBERRY KETCHUP

A must-have item on your pantry shelves, this is tasty served with poultry or game.

Equipment

stainless steel saucepan
food processor
cheesecloth (muslin)
string
tongs
ladle
storage jar
label

Ingredients

12 oz (375 g) cranberries

1 large red (Spanish) onion, chopped

1 cinnamon stick

$1/2$ teaspoon mustard seeds

$1/2$ teaspoon whole allspice

$1/2$ teaspoon black peppercorns

$1/2$ cup (4 fl oz/125 ml) water

1 cup (8 oz/250 g) sugar

$1/2$ cup (4 fl oz/125 ml) cider vinegar

$1 1/2$ teaspoons salt

*Finished Quantity
2 cups (16 fl oz/500 ml)*

1 **BOIL CRANBERRIES AND ONION** In a saucepan, cover the cranberries and onion with water and bring to a boil. Lower heat, cover, and simmer for 20 minutes.

2 **PURÉE** Transfer the cranberry and onion mixture to a food processor and process until smooth. Place a clean dish towel over the processor bowl to prevent burns from the hot mixture. Test for smoothness; if there are any skins remaining, process again.

3 **RETURN TO HEAT** Spoon the mixture into the saucepan and cook over a medium heat for 20 minutes, until reduced to 2 cups (16 fl oz/500 ml).

4 **MAKE SPICE BAG** Place the cinnamon, mustard seeds, allspice, and peppercorns in a cheesecloth square, and tie with string.

5 **ADD REMAINING INGREDIENTS AND COOK** Add the spice bag, water, sugar, vinegar, and salt to the mixture in the saucepan. Cook slowly over a low heat until the mixture is very thick, 10–20 minutes. Stir frequently being careful not to let the mixture burn.

6 **REMOVE SPICE BAG AND BOTTLE** Use a pair of tongs to remove the spice bag from the saucepan, discard. Ladle the ketchup into a sterilized jar (see page 18).

7 **SEAL** Cap tightly, and label if desired. Refrigerate for up to 2 weeks.

SHOPPING ADVICE

🌿 *If fresh cranberries are unavailable, an equivalent amount of frozen cranberries may be substituted.*
🌿 *Always purchase spices, such as cinnamon sticks, as you need them, so that they retain their freshness.*

MUSHROOM KETCHUP

The tangy, unusual flavors of this ketchup are compatible with pork and chicken.

Equipment

sharp knife
chopping board
ovenproof bowl
aluminum foil
cheesecloth (muslin)
stainless steel saucepan
ladle
strainer
large mixing bowl
storage jars
water-bath canner
labels

Ingredients

3 lb (1.5 kg) mushrooms

5 tablespoons salt

²/₃ cup (5 fl oz/155 ml) cider vinegar

2-inch (5-cm) piece ginger

5 whole cloves

1 teaspoon whole allspice

1 teaspoon whole black peppercorns

1 cinnamon stick

Finished Quantity
1 quart (1 l)

1 CHOP MUSHROOMS Coarsely chop the mushrooms and stems.

2 COVER WITH SALT In an ovenproof bowl, layer the mushrooms. Sprinkle each layer with the salt, cover, and let stand in a cool place for 5 days.

3 MIX DAILY Stir the mushrooms each day. Retain the liquid that forms from the mushrooms.

4 BAKE Cover the bowl with aluminum foil and bake for 1¹/₂ hours at 300°F (150°C/Gas 2).

5 STRAIN Let the mushrooms cool, and then press the mushrooms through several layers of cheesecloth into a saucepan. Discard the mushrooms.

6 ADD REMAINING INGREDIENTS Stir in the vinegar, slice the ginger, and add along with the spices. Bring to a boil. Simmer, uncovered, until the liquid is reduced by half, about 45 minutes.

7 STRAIN AGAIN Press the mixture through a strainer lined with cheesecloth into a mixing bowl.

8 BOTTLE Ladle the ketchup into sterilized jars (see page 18) leaving 1/4 inch (0.5 cm) headspace.

9 PROCESS AND STORE Clean the jar rims and seal. Process in a water-bath canner (see page 41) for 30 minutes. Remove the jars from the canner, let cool, and label, if desired. This will keep for 6 months in a cool, dark place, and for 1 week in the refrigerator after opening.

SPICED AND SEEDED MUSTARDS

There are three types of mustard seed: black, brown, and white (sometimes called yellow). In America, the tiny and hard black and brown seeds are scarce, while the larger and milder white seeds are more plentiful. Black and brown seeds are used in hotter European mustards, but white seeds generally are used in the milder American ones.

The first grinding and combining of the mustard seeds with liquid produces the most intense, pungent flavor. Make your sauce fresh each meal if you want the most dramatic flavor. For a milder taste, a cooked mustard made with vinegar, wine, sugar, or salt is in order. Add the crushed seeds or powder during the first minutes of cooking time and the intensity of the mustard flavor will be there at the end, but not the strong, hot sensation.

Several tablespoons of good olive oil and a few drops of aged vinegar whisked into a pungent but delicate prepared mustard create a lovely, smooth dressing to complement any salad greens. Experiment with commercially prepared mustards, from smooth to grainy, hot to mild, and before long you'll want to try your own ideas for flavorings. Homemade mustards are easy and inexpensive to make, and with experimentation the combinations are limitless.

HOMEMADE HERBED MUSTARD

This is a terrific accompaniment to chicken, pork, or fish. Before you prepare the mustard, fill the jars with boiling water and let stand for 10 minutes. Pour out the water and invert the jars onto clean dish towels.

Equipment

stainless steel saucepan
electric beater
ladle
small storage jars
labels

Ingredients

1/3 cup (3 oz/90 g) white mustard seeds, ground

1 teaspoon mustard powder

1/2 cup (4 fl oz/125 ml) dry white wine

1/4 cup (2 fl oz/60 ml) champagne vinegar

1 tablespoon brown sugar

2 teaspoons dried or 1 tablespoon fresh herbs (basil or oregano)

Finished Quantity
1 cup (8 oz/250 g)

1 HEAT MUSTARD, WINE, AND VINEGAR In a saucepan over low heat, combine the ground seeds with the mustard powder, wine, and vinegar. Cook, covered, for 5–7 minutes. Stir occasionally, checking frequently to insure that it doesn't burn.

2 BLEND UNTIL SMOOTH While still over the heat, using an electric beater, blend the mustard until smooth.

3 ADD BROWN SUGAR AND STIR IN HERBS Stir in the brown sugar, allowing the mixture to simmer, uncovered, over low heat for 5–7 minutes. Stir in the herbs.

4 COOL, BOTTLE, AND STORE Let the mixture cool. Pack into small, sterilized jars (see page 18), and label, or serve it warm immediately after making. The sauce will thicken as it cools. Keep refrigerated for 3–4 weeks.

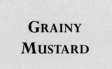

GRAINY MUSTARD

Add 1 teaspoon of this mustard to olive oil and vinegar for a wonderful dressing over tossed salad greens.

Equipment

mixing bowl
mortar and pestle
strainer
stainless steel saucepan
ladle
small storage jars
labels

Ingredients

1³/4 cups (14 fl oz/440 ml) white wine vinegar

2 small onions, sliced

8 sprigs fresh tarragon

¹/2 cup (4 fl oz/125 ml) water

¹/2 cup (4 oz/125 g) white mustard seeds

3 tablespoons mustard powder

1 teaspoon black pepper

2 teaspoons soy sauce

1 tablespoon honey

1 teaspoon turmeric

Finished Quantity
2 cups (1 lb/500 g)

1 MAKE INFUSION Combine the vinegar, sliced onions, and tarragon in a mixing bowl. Bring the ¹/2 cup (4 fl oz/125 ml) of water to a boil, pour over the ingredients in the bowl, cover, and leave to marinate for 3 hours.

2 GRIND MUSTARD SEEDS Using a mortar and pestle, or a food processor, pulverize the mustard seeds.

3 STRAIN Pour the vinegar mixture through a strainer into a saucepan.

4 **ADD REMAINING INGREDIENTS** Stir in the pulverized mustard seeds, mustard powder, pepper, soy sauce, honey, and turmeric, and mix well. Bring to a boil and simmer for about 5 minutes, stirring occasionally. Taste and add a little water to tame down the heat if necessary.

SERVING TIPS

🌿 Smear chicken pieces with this tangy concoction, and cover with fresh breadcrumbs. Bake the chicken in a preheated 350°F (180°C/Gas 4) oven until golden, 30–40 minutes. Delicious!

🌿 Like all mustards, this version contains very few calories, so forget the mayonnaise and instead be lavish with this spread.

6 **SEAL AND STORE** Cap tightly, label, and refrigerate for 3–4 weeks. Let the mustard thicken for 24 hours before using.

5 **BOTTLE** Ladle into small sterilized jars (see page 18).

Mustard with horseradish makes cold cuts a treat.

1 PREPARE MUSTARD
In a bowl, combine the mustard and water, stirring until smooth. Let stand for 2 hours.

2 MAKE INFUSION In a saucepan, combine all of the remaining ingredients except the horseradish and boil until reduced to 3 cups (24 fl oz/750 ml), about 30 minutes.

3 STRAIN Press the mixture through a strainer and discard all the solid remains.

5 ADD HORSERADISH Remove from the heat and stir in the horseradish.

6 BOTTLE, SEAL, AND STORE Ladle the mustard into small sterilized jars (see page 18). Cap tightly, label, and refrigerate. This recipe will keep for up to 6 weeks.

4 ADD MUSTARD MIXTURE Place the infusion in the top of a double boiler and add the mustard mixture. Cook, stirring occasionally, until reduced to 2 cups (16 fl oz / 500 ml), about 45 minutes.

TARRAGON MUSTARD

Try basil or thyme as a substitute for the tarragon for a different range of flavors. Serve warm or cold as a complement to chicken, pork, or lamb.

Equipment

stainless steel saucepan
storage jar
label

Ingredients

¹/₂ cup (4 oz / 125 g) coarsely ground prepared mustard

1 teaspoon mustard powder

¹/₂ cup (4 fl oz / 125 ml) dry white wine

¹/₄ cup (2 fl oz / 60 ml) white wine vinegar

1 tablespoon brown sugar

¹/₂ teaspoon salt

2 teaspoons dried tarragon

Finished Quantity
1 cup (8 oz / 250 g)

1 COOK FIRST FOUR INGREDIENTS In a saucepan on a low heat, combine the mustards, wine, and vinegar. Cover and cook for about 20 minutes, stirring frequently and being careful not to burn.

2 ADD SUGAR AND SALT Stir in the brown sugar and salt and allow to cook, uncovered, for another 3–4 minutes.

3 ADD TARRAGON Remove the saucepan from the heat and add the tarragon.

4 BOTTLE AND STORE Spoon the mustard into a sterilized jar (see page 18); seal and label. It will keep for 1 month stored in the refrigerator, but is best served immediately as it loses some of the tartness as it ages. The mixture will thicken as it cools.

LIME MUSTARD WITH CORIANDER

Buy strongly aromatic juicy
limes (scratch the skin and
sniff) from midsummer to fall
for best results.

Equipment

mixing bowl
food processor
serving spoon
storage jars
labels

Ingredients

2¹/8 cups (17 oz/530 g)
white mustard seeds, ground

2 tablespoons mustard
powder

¹/2 cup (4 fl oz/125 ml)
water

²/3 cup (5 fl oz/155 ml)
white wine vinegar

¹/4 cup (3 fl oz/90 ml) honey

¹/4 cup (2 oz/60 g) sugar

2 teaspoons salt

2 teaspoons ground
coriander seeds

grated zest (rind) 1 lime

2¹/4 tablespoons lime juice

Finished Quantity
2 cups (1 lb/500 g)

1 **MIX IN WATER** In a bowl,
combine the ground mustard
seeds and mustard powder
with the water. Allow to
marry for 3 hours.

2 **PURÉE**
Transfer the
mixture to a food
processor, and
gradually
add the other
ingredients
except the lime
juice while
processing.

3 **ADD LIME JUICE**
Sample the mixture,
adding enough of the
lime juice to make a
smooth mixture.

4 **BOTTLE, SEAL, AND
STORE** Spoon into small
sterilized jars (see page 18).
Cap the jars tightly, and
label. Store in the
refrigerator
for several
months.

GERMAN MUSTARD

A grainy texture adds to the pleasure of this mustard.

Equipment

mixing bowl
stainless steel saucepan
ladle
strainer
food processor
double boiler
storage jar
label

Ingredients

¹/4 cup (2 oz / 60 g) brown mustard seeds, ground

5 tablespoons mustard powder

¹/3 cup (3 fl oz / 90 ml) water

³/4 cup (6 fl oz / 185 ml) champagne vinegar

2 tablespoons cold water

2 large onions, sliced

1 tablespoon honey

1 teaspoon molasses

2 cloves garlic, halved

¹/4 teaspoon each dill seed, cinnamon, allspice, cloves

Finished Quantity
1 cup (8 oz / 250 g)

1 PREPARE MUSTARD SEEDS
In a bowl, combine the mustard seeds and mustard powder. Heat the ¹/3 cup (3 fl oz / 90 ml) of water and add with ¹/4 cup (2 fl oz / 60 ml) of the vinegar. Let stand for 3 hours so the bitterness of the mustard disappears.

2 MAKE INFUSION Meanwhile, put all the remaining ingredients in a saucepan and boil for 1 minute.

3 SET ASIDE AND COOL Remove the pan from the heat, cover, and let stand for 1 hour.

SPICED AND SEEDED MUSTARDS

4 **STRAIN** Press the infusion through a strainer into a food processor. Discard all solid remains.

5 **ADD MUSTARD SEED MIXTURE AND PROCESS** Ladle in the reserved mustard mixture and process until coarse.

6 **SIMMER** Put in the top of a double boiler and cook over simmering water for 25 minutes, or until thickened. Remove from heat.

7 **BOTTLE, SEAL, AND STORE** Ladle into a sterilized jar (see page 18). Cap tightly and label. The mustard will thicken as it cools. Store in the refrigerator for about 1 month.

This mustard measures up to spicy sausages for a winter meal. Add some sauerkraut for an incredibly easy menu. Should you find it too hot, the mustard becomes milder the longer it is stored.

Equipment

mixing bowl
whisk
ladle
storage jars
labels

Ingredients

¹/₂ cup (4 fl oz/125 ml) cold water

2 cups (1 lb/500 g) mustard powder

¹/₂ cup (4 fl oz/125 ml) cider vinegar

¹/₂ cup (4 fl oz/125 ml) vegetable oil

¹/₂ cup (3 oz/90 g) firmly packed brown sugar

pinch of salt

Finished Quantity
2 cups (1 lb/500 g)

1 COMBINE WATER AND MUSTARD Gradually whisk the water into the mustard powder, beating out all the lumps. Let rest for 15 minutes. Any bitterness from the mustard powder will disappear during this time.

2 ADD VINEGAR AND OIL Whisk in the vinegar and oil, mixing until smooth.

3 ADD REMAINING INGREDIENTS Mix in the brown sugar and salt and stir until smooth.

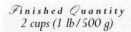

4 BOTTLE, SEAL, AND STORE Ladle the mustard into small sterilized jars (see page 18). Cap tightly, label, and store in the refrigerator for up to 1–2 months.

SAUCES
AND SALSAS

*T*oday, sauces from around the world enhance and complement the flavor of a dish rather than mask it. This was not the case long ago, when much of the food people ate was rancid or spoiled due to lack of refrigeration, and numerous sauces and herbs were used to hide that fact.

Salsa is the Spanish word for sauce. In the past it generally referred to a fresh tomato and onion sauce used as a dip for corn chips. Now you find salsa recipes based on cooked or uncooked tomatoes and other chopped ripe fruits such as avocados and pineapple, some garnished with citrus slices, with the finished product made for dipping or garnishing fresh vegetables, fruits, and meat.

These recipes are not meant to be entrée (main course) sauces, but fulfill their purpose as "dress-ups" for more zestful dining. They can be served hot, cold, or at room temperature. They may be added during cooking or at serving time. Ideas are as simple as Piquant Sauce, used as a dip, or as complicated as a unique, spicey marinade for lamb, pork, or chicken.

PERFECT GARDEN PESTO

Fresh herbs such as tarragon, parsley, or cilantro (fresh coriander) may be substituted for or added with the basil. Parsley is a natural choice to supplement the basil when cold weather eliminates many of the other herb choices.

Equipment

food processor
storage jar
label
ice cube trays

Ingredients

2 cups (2 oz / 60 g) fresh basil (or parsley, tarragon, or cilantro / fresh coriander)

3 cloves garlic

1/2 cup (4 fl oz / 125 ml) olive oil

salt to taste

3/4 cup (3 oz / 90 g) freshly grated Parmesan cheese

2 tablespoons (1 1/2 oz / 45 g) butter

3 tablespoons pine nuts

Finished Quantity
2 cups (1 lb / 500 g)

1 **PURÉE HERBS, GARLIC, OLIVE OIL, AND SALT** Place the herbs in a food processor, add the garlic, drizzle in the olive oil (reserving 1 teaspoon), and purée until smooth. Add salt to taste.

2 **ADD PARMESAN, BUTTER, AND PINE NUTS** Add the Parmesan cheese, butter, and pine nuts and process until smooth.

3 **BOTTLE AND STORE** Pour into a sterilized jar (see page 18) and cover with a thin layer of olive oil. Alternatively, you can freeze the pesto, in individual blocks in an ice cube tray, before adding the Parmesan cheese.

SERVING SUGGESTIONS

❧ Add a spoonful or a cube of pesto to canned tomato soup.
❧ Spice up leftover French bread by toasting and spreading it with pesto, then topping it with fresh tomato and mozzarella slices.
❧ Use pesto "straight" as a dip for fresh platters of raw vegetables.

BARBECUE SAUCE

The traditional favorite!

Equipment

large skillet (frying pan)
food processor
mixing spoon
tongs
ladle
storage jars
water-bath canner
labels

Ingredients

24 large, ripe tomatoes

3 stalks celery

2 medium onions

3¹/₂ bell peppers (capsicums)

1 teaspoon peppercorns,
tied in cheesecloth (muslin)

2–3 fresh red chilies, seeded

1 cup (8 oz / 250 g) sugar

3 cloves garlic, minced

1 tablespoon mustard
powder

1 tablespoon paprika

1 tablespoon salt

1 cup (8 fl oz / 250 ml)
cider vinegar

Finished Quantity
2 quarts (2 l)

1 COMBINE FIRST FOUR INGREDIENTS Peel and chop the tomatoes, celery, onions, and bell peppers. Heat a skillet on low and add the tomatoes, celery, onions, and bell peppers. Sweat slowly until soft, about 30 minutes.

2 PURÉE Transfer to a food processor, and purée until smooth.

3 COOK AND THEN ADD REMAINING INGREDIENTS Return the mixture to the skillet and cook until reduced by half, about 40 minutes, stirring occasionally and being careful not to let the bottom of the pan stick. Stir in the remaining ingredients and cook for another 1¹/₂ hours, stirring frequently, making sure the sauce does not burn.

4 REMOVE SPICE BAG

Using a pair of tongs, remove the peppercorn bag.

5 BOTTLE

Ladle the sauce into sterilized jars (see page 18), leaving ¼ inch (0.5 cm) headspace.

6 SEAL

Clean the jar rims and insure the jars are tightly sealed.

7 PROCESS AND THEN STORE

Place the rack in the bottom of the water-bath canner. Half-fill the canner with hot or boiling water. Lower the jars into the canner, insuring that they do not touch one another, the bottom, or the sides. Add more hot water to cover tops of jars by 2 inches (5 cm). Bring to a rolling boil, cover, and process for 20 minutes. Remove the jars from the canner using a jar lifter. Place on clean dish towels to cool, allowing space between each jar. After 24 hours remove the screw rings; and label. Keep for 9 months–1 year on the pantry shelf. Store in the refrigerator, after opening, for up to 2 weeks.

HEADSPACE

When canning, it is essential to leave space between the top of the food and the rim of the storage container to enable a vacuum to form. Each recipe has a specified amount of headspace indicated because if too much or too little is allowed a seal will not form, causing the food to spoil.

PEANUT SAUCE FOR SATAY

Serve this as a dip for vegetables, pork, beef, or chicken, or as a delicious cold dressing for Chinese noodles.

Equipment

*microwave-safe bowl
microwave oven or
double boiler
mixing spoon
storage container
label*

Ingredients

1 cup (8 oz/250 g) chunky peanut butter

4 fresh red chilies, seeded and sliced

2 cloves garlic, minced

2 tablespoons sugar

1 teaspoon cayenne pepper

5 tablespoons fresh lime juice

5 tablespoons low sodium dark soy sauce

3 tablespoons groundnut (peanut) oil

2 tablespoons water

*Finished Quantity
2¹/₂ cups (1¹/₄ lb/625 g)*

1 COMBINE INGREDIENTS Mix all of the ingredients in a bowl.

2 COOK Heat the sauce on high for 1¹/₂–2 minutes in the microwave, or place in the top of a double boiler, cover, and cook for 5–10 minutes.

3 REMOVE AND STIR Remove the sauce from heat source and stir until well blended. The sauce should be of a dipping consistency. Add more water, if necessary.

4 USE IMMEDIATELY OR COVER AND STORE Use immediately, or transfer the sauce to a sterilized container (see page 18), seal, and label, if desired. Store the mixture in the refrigerator for up to 1 week.

PIQUANT SAUCE

Serve this sauce with smoked meat or fish, or as a sensational party dip for raw vegetables. You can substitute low- or non-fat sour cream and 2 tablespoons of cream-style prepared horseradish.

Equipment

mixing bowl
storage container

Ingredients

2 cups (16 fl oz / 500 ml) sour cream

4 tablespoons freshly grated horseradish

6 tablespoons capers, drained

4 drops hot pepper sauce (such as Tabasco)

Finished Quantity
2 cups (16 fl oz / 500 ml)

1 **MAKE SAUCE** Mix all of the ingredients together in a bowl.

2 **REFRIGERATE** Place in a sterilized container (see page 18) in the refrigerator for 2 hours. Refrigerate for up to 1 week.

JEZEBEL SAUCE

Devilishly sweet, hot, and surprising, like Jezebel in the book of Kings, you'll want to serve this with pork and ham, or as a garnish for cream cheese and crackers.

Equipment

mixing bowl
storage jar
label

Ingredients

2 cups (1 1/2 lb / 750 g) pineapple preserves

2 cups (1 1/2 lb / 750 g) apple jelly

2 tablespoons prepared horseradish

2 teaspoons Creole mustard

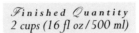

Finished Quantity
1 quart (1 l)

1 **PREPARE SAUCE** Combine all of the ingredients in a bowl and stir well.

2 **STORE** Use immediately or transfer to a labeled storage jar. Refrigerate for up to 2 weeks.

HORSERADISH BUTTER

This is delicious added to new boiled potatoes or broiled (grilled) fish.

Equipment

mixing bowl
fork
spatula
ice cube trays

Ingredients

1/2 cup (4 oz/125 g) butter, at room temperature

2 tablespoons freshly grated horseradish or 3 tablespoons prepared horseradish, drained

1 teaspoon freshly ground black pepper

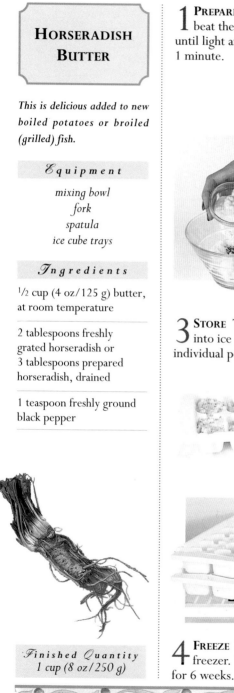

Finished Quantity
1 cup (8 oz/250 g)

1 PREPARE BUTTER In a bowl, beat the butter with a fork until light and fluffy, about 1 minute.

2 ADD REMAINING INGREDIENTS Add the horseradish and pepper, and stir well.

3 STORE Transfer the butter into ice cube trays for individual portions.

4 FREEZE Place the trays in the freezer. The butter will keep for 6 weeks.

CUMBERLAND SAUCE

A flavorsome accompaniment to pork, turkey, and broiled (grilled) chicken, this recipe is a traditional favorite.

Equipment

stainless steel saucepan
mixing spoon
ladle
storage container

Ingredients

2 cups (1 lb 6 oz/690 g) redcurrant jelly

4 tablespoons thinly sliced orange zest (rind)

1/4 cup (2 fl oz/60 ml) orange juice concentrate

2 tablespoons sugar

1 tablespoon mustard powder

1 1/2 teaspoons ground ginger

1/4 teaspoon salt

1/4 teaspoon pepper

1 cup (8 fl oz/250 ml) dry port

Finished Quantity
3 cups (24 fl oz/750 ml)

1 PREPARE SAUCE In a saucepan over a low heat, cook all of the ingredients except the port for 2 minutes. Stir occasionally, being careful not to burn.

2 SIMMER Add the port and simmer for another 2 minutes or until thickened. Remove the zest.

3 BOTTLE Ladle the sauce into a sterilized container (see page 18) and seal.

4 STORE Cool the sauce and refrigerate for up to 2 weeks.

PREPARATION TIP
You can easily double or triple this recipe and make this sauce just before Christmas. Packed in decorative jars, Cumberland Sauce makes a delicious gift for your friends and neighbors.

SUSAN'S SATAY MARINADE

This is a special concoction made by my friend Susan. It is delicious with lamb, pork, or chicken.

Equipment

mixing bowl
wooden skewers soaked in water for at least 1 hour

Ingredients

¹/₂ onion

2 cloves garlic

1 teaspoon grated ginger

1 cup (8 fl oz/250 ml) soy sauce

¹/₂ cup (4 fl oz/125 ml) coconut milk

¹/₄ cup (2 fl oz/60 ml) dry sherry

¹/₄ cup (2 fl oz/60 ml) sesame oil

3 tablespoons lime juice

1 tablespoon chili paste

2 tablespoons tamarind paste

2¹/₂ lb (1.25 kg) chicken breast fillets

Finished Quantity
2 cups (16 fl oz/500 ml)

1 PREPARE MARINADE AND MAKE KEBABS
Grate the onion and crush the garlic. Combine with all of the other ingredients, except the chicken, in a bowl. Cut the chicken into strips and thread onto skewers.

2 MARINATE
Place the skewers in the marinade ensuring that they are covered with the sauce. Refrigerate for up to 24 hours.

3 SERVE Broil (grill) or barbecue the skewers, and serve with a satay sauce (see page 42). The marinade can also be placed in a labeled storage container and frozen for up to 1 month, if desired.

DARK AND TANGY CHILI SAUCE

Pour this over roasting chicken pieces, serve as a garnish for burgers, or use it as a dip for fresh vegetables or corn chips as part of a spicy picnic or party menu.

Equipment

food processor
stainless steel saucepan
serving spoon
freezer containers
labels

Ingredients

30–40 ripe tomatoes

5–7 medium onions

8 green bell peppers (capsicums)

5 tablespoons brown sugar

3 tablespoons salt

5 cups (1¼ quarts/1.25 l) cider vinegar

1 tablespoon each cloves, grated ginger, nutmeg, ground cinnamon

pinch allspice

Finished Quantity
About 5 quarts (5 l)

1 PROCESS TOMATOES, ONIONS, AND PEPPERS In a food processor, chop the tomatoes, onions, and peppers to a coarse consistency.

2 HEAT Transfer the tomato mixture to a saucepan. Add the brown sugar, salt, and vinegar. Cook for 2 hours over low heat, stirring frequently and being careful not to burn.

PREPARATION TIP

❧ Nutmeg is best bought whole and grated as you need it; the flavor is infinitely superior to bought ground nutmeg. You can either use a special grinder, or grate it on a fine grater.
❧ There are two varieties of cinnamon available: Cassia cinnamon is more pungent than Ceylon cinnamon and is a dark, reddish brown color.

3 ADD REMAINING INGREDIENTS
Add the spices and cook for about 2 more hours, stirring frequently.

5 SEAL AND FREEZE
Seal the containers, label, and freeze. Store for up to 6 months, thawing in the refrigerator when required.

4 PLACE IN CONTAINERS
Spoon the sauce into clean freezer containers.

TANGY FRUIT SALSA

Use this colorful concoction as a delicious side dish for lamb, pork, or chicken, or as an accompaniment to freshly sautéed scallops.

Equipment
mixing bowl
mixing spoon

Ingredients

¹/₂ pineapple, finely chopped

¹/₂ red bell pepper (capsicum), finely chopped

¹/₂ yellow bell pepper (capsicum), finely chopped

1 small red (Spanish) onion, finely chopped

1 jalapeño chili, seeded and finely chopped

juice 1 lime

1¹/₂ teaspoons brown sugar

Finished Quantity
2 cups (14 oz / 440 g)

1 COMBINE INGREDIENTS
Combine all of the ingredients, mixing well.

2 REFRIGERATE AND STORE
Cover and store in the refrigerator for 3 hours before serving. This salsa can also be refrigerated for 2–4 days.

FRESH TERIYAKI SAUCE

This is great as a handy stir-fry sauce, marinade for chicken, beef, or pork, or as a dipping sauce for raw vegetables. It is also very good served over Oriental noodles.

Equipment

storage jar
label

Ingredients

1 cup (8 fl oz / 250 ml) Japanese soy sauce

1 cup (8 fl oz / 250 ml) mirin (sweet Japanese rice wine)

1 tablespoon rice vinegar

1 tablespoon light brown sugar

4 teaspoons peeled and finely minced fresh ginger

4 cloves garlic, minced

Finished Quantity
2 cups (16 fl oz / 500 ml)

1 COMBINE INGREDIENTS Mix all of the ingredients in a sterilized jar (see page 18).

2 SEAL AND STORE Cap the jar tightly, and label if desired. Let stand for 2–3 hours before using or store in the refrigerator for 2–3 weeks.

JALAPEÑO–CRANBERRY SAUCE

Serve this sauce warm with lamb, chicken, or pork, or for a zestful winter meal, use to garnish sautéed turkey breasts. Serve cold with cream cheese and crackers.

Equipment

stainless steel saucepan
storage container
label

Ingredients

1 lb (500 g) canned whole berry cranberry sauce

1/2 cup (4 fl oz / 125 ml) apple jelly

1 jalapeño chili, finely chopped

SERVING TIP
This sauce may also be stored in the freezer for 6 weeks. The mixture will thicken as it cools.

Finished Quantity
2 cups (16 fl oz / 500 ml)

1 PREPARE SAUCE Combine all of the ingredients in a saucepan. Cook slowly over low heat until the jelly melts, about 5 minutes, stirring all the while so the sauce does not burn.

2 COVER AND STORE Pour into a sterilized container (see page 18), label if desired, and refrigerate for up to 10 days, or pour into a jug to serve.

TOMATO SALSA

You'll never have any of this left over, especially when serving it to hungry teenagers.

Equipment

food processor
storage container
label

Ingredients

4 large ripe tomatoes, roughly chopped

3 fresh jalapeño chilies, seeded and split

6–8 green (spring) onions, chopped

2 cloves garlic

8 sprigs cilantro (fresh coriander), stems removed

salt to taste

1 PROCESS TOMATOES, CHILIES, ONIONS, AND HERBS

In a food processor, chop the tomatoes, chilies, onions, garlic, and cilantro to a coarse texture.

2 ADD SALT

Stir in the salt, mixing well, and serve immediately or store, as is, in the refrigerator for 2 days.

3 STORAGE

If there is any salsa left over, transfer to a skillet and simmer for 5 minutes. This brief cooking will allow the salsa to be kept longer. Place in a storage container, label if desired, and keep in the refrigerator for an additional week, or frozen for up to a month.

Finished Quantity
2 cups (1 lb / 500 g)

CHERRY TOMATO SALSA

Serve this as a spicy dip for tortilla chips, or as a topping for warm crab meat, shredded fresh spinach, and cheese.

Equipment

food processor
mixing bowl
storage container
label

Ingredients

1 lb (500 g) cherry tomatoes

1 large shallot, minced

1 clove garlic, minced

2 tablespoons chopped cilantro (fresh coriander)

1 tablespoon white wine vinegar

salt to taste

pepper to taste

2 teaspoons fresh lime juice

2 jalapeño chilies, seeded and chopped

Finished Quantity
2 cups (12 oz / 375 g)

1 PROCESS TOMATOES
In a food processor, process the tomatoes to a coarse consistency.

2 COMBINE ALL INGREDIENTS
Transfer the tomatoes with their juice to a bowl and mix in the remaining ingredients.

3 COVER Cover the bowl or transfer the salsa to a sterilized storage container (see page 18), refrigerate, and let the flavors marry for at least 2 hours.

4 STORE Label the container, if desired, and refrigerate for 2–3 days.

TOMATILLO SALSA

This green salsa is delicious with barbecued pork, or as a dip for taco chips.

Equipment

food processor
stainless steel saucepan
mixing spoon
serving bowl
label

Ingredients

3 jalapeño chilies, halved and seeded

1 medium onion, quartered

1 clove garlic, quartered

2 tablespoons minced cilantro (fresh coriander)

20 tomatillos, husked, washed, and heated until tender to make 2¹/₂ cups (22 oz/690 g)

¹/₂ teaspoon sugar

salt to taste

pepper to taste

2 tablespoons olive oil

Finished Quantity
3 cups (2 lb/1 kg)

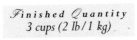

1 PROCESS CHILIES, ONION, AND GARLIC Finely chop the chilies, onion, and garlic in a food processor.

2 ADD CILANTRO, TOMATILLOS, SUGAR, SALT, AND PEPPER Add all of the other ingredients except the oil and process again.

3 HEAT OLIVE OIL AND ADD PURÉED INGREDIENTS In a saucepan, heat the olive oil and add the puréed ingredients. Cook over a medium heat for about 5 minutes, being careful not to burn.

4 PLACE IN CONTAINER AND STORE Transfer the salsa to a serving bowl; if not using immediately, cover, label if desired, and store in the refrigerator for 6–7 days.

GREG MORENO'S MEXICAN SALSA

After much experimenting, cooking, and tasting, a great Mexican friend of mine, Greg Moreno, has perfected this combination of ingredients.

ℰquipment

skillet (frying pan)
tongs
sharp knife
chopping board
mixing bowl
mixing spoon
storage jar
label

ℐngredients

6 ripe medium tomatoes

2 green jalapeño chilies, seeded and chopped if desired

4 sprigs fresh oregano

1/2 medium onion, minced

1/4 tablespoon cilantro (fresh coriander)

2 cloves garlic, minced

salt to taste

Finished Quantity
2 cups (1 lb / 500 g)

1 SKIN TOMATOES Put the tomatoes in a hot skillet to crack the skins. Cook for 2–4 minutes to reduce the tomato juice slightly. Cool and remove the skins.

2 CHOP TOMATOES Finely chop the tomatoes.

3 ADD REMAINING INGREDIENTS In a bowl, combine the remaining ingredients with the tomatoes, mixing well.

4 BOTTLE Spoon the salsa into a sterilized jar (see page 18).

5 SEAL AND STORE Cover securely and label, if desired. Keep for 3–5 days in the refrigerator.

54

DIPS AND DRESSINGS

$\mathcal{D}$ips and dressings can quickly enhance a plain platter of raw vegetables, a bland bowl of salad greens, or a steamy mound of otherwise unadorned white rice. Many of these dips are extremely easy to prepare and will spice up a simple meal. Most of these recipes can either be used immediately after preparing, or stored in the refrigerator for use within several days or a week or two.

When preparing any food in the kitchen, it is always important to start with clean hands and equipment. Follow the directions exactly as written in the recipe. There are no exceptions to this rule. Improperly sterilized jars all too often harbor potentially dangerous bacteria.

Clean jars with no chips or cracks are essential. Never re-use lids, although last season's rings and jars in good condition can be re-used. Never use old food-stuff jars in place of quality commercial canning jars. Wash the storage jars in hot, soapy water and fill with boiling water to scald them. Dry the jars and keep them warm until ready to fill.

For short-term storage in the refrigerator, use plastic containers with lids that have been washed in hot, soapy water and then scalded with boiling water.

CLASSIC DRESSING

This makes a wonderfully light summertime favorite. Only the cook will know it is low in calories; the guests will just think it is delicious. This dressing can be varied by using different combinations of herbs.

Equipment

*food processor or blender
storage jar
label*

Ingredients

¹/₂ cup (¹/₂ oz/15 g)
fresh parsley

4 small green (spring) onions

1¹/₂ teaspoons fresh tarragon

1 tablespoon anchovy paste

¹/₂ cup (4 oz/125 g)
low-fat cottage cheese

¹/₄ cup (2 fl oz/60 ml)
non-fat yogurt

2 tablespoons whole-egg
mayonnaise

2 tablespoons lemon juice

Finished Quantity
1 cup (8 fl oz/250 ml)

1 **BLEND PARSLEY AND ONIONS** Combine the parsley in a food processor or blender with the onions cut into ¹/₂-inch (1-cm) lengths, using 3 inches (7.5 cm) of the top green parts. Add the tarragon, anchovy paste, cottage cheese, yogurt, mayonnaise, and lemon juice.

2 **PURÉE MIXTURE AND POUR INTO JAR** Process until mixture is completely puréed. The dressing will be thin. Pour into a sterilized jar (see page 18).

3 **CHILL IN REFRIGERATOR** Cover, label if desired, and chill in the refrigerator for at least 30 minutes before using. The dressing can be refrigerated for up to 2 days.

SERVING TIP

The dressing will thicken when chilled and it is at its best if served the next day. You can serve it as a low-fat dip for raw vegetables, a fresh and appealing salad dressing, or as a tangy accompaniment for broiled (grilled) fish.

Olive Aïoli

Full-flavored and aromatic, this dark, pungent sauce is the perfect partner to boiled new potatoes. A sprig of rosemary can be added to the finished potato salad for decoration. Regular aïoli can be made by omitting both the olives and the rosemary.

Equipment

food processor
serving spoon
storage jar
label

Ingredients

3 cloves garlic

3 tablespoons puréed, oil-cured kalamata olives

1 teaspoon chopped fresh rosemary

¹/₂ cup (4 fl oz / 125 ml) whole-egg mayonnaise

2–3 tablespoons olive oil

¹/₂ teaspoon fresh lemon juice

Finished Quantity
³/₄ cup (6 fl oz / 185 ml)

1 **PROCESS GARLIC, OLIVE PURÉE, ROSEMARY, AND MAYONNAISE; ADD OIL** Combine the garlic, olive purée, rosemary, and mayonnaise in a food processor and process until smooth. Add the olive oil a few drops at a time until the mixture is smooth.

2 **ADD LEMON JUICE** Squeeze the lemon juice into the mixture and continue to process for a few seconds.

3 **TRANSFER TO JAR** Transfer the aïoli to a sterilized jar (see page 18).

4 **COVER AND REFRIGERATE** Cover or seal the jar and label, if desired. Refrigerate until required. The mixture thickens when it is chilled. If the mixture separates, add another tablespoon of mayonnaise and beat for a few minutes until it amalgamates. Keeps for up to 1 week in the refrigerator.

TOMATO DRESSING

This light tomato dressing makes a perfect salad when poured over slices of tomatoes, hard-cooked eggs, diced onions, and capers.

Equipment

storage jar
label

Ingredients

1 medium tomato, seeded, drained, and finely chopped

$^1/_2$ cup (4 fl oz / 125 ml) olive oil

2 tablespoons cider vinegar

2 teaspoons honey

1 clove garlic, minced

1 teaspoon soy sauce

$^1/_4$ teaspoon paprika

salt

small dash hot pepper sauce (such as Tabasco)

Finished Quantity
$^3/_4$ *cup (6 fl oz / 185 ml)*

1 COMBINE INGREDIENTS
Combine all of the ingredients in a sterilized jar (see page 18) with a tight-fitting lid.

2 COVER AND SHAKE
Cover and shake well. Label, if desired.

3 REFRIGERATE
Chill until required. This recipe will keep in the refrigerator for about 1 week.

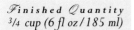

A royal complement to spring salad greens. Happily, the calories are also missing!

𝓔quipment

food processor
spoon
storage jar
label

𝓘ngredients

¹/₂ cup (1 oz / 30 g) chopped fresh parsley

3 green (spring) onions, chopped

³/₄ teaspoon dried oregano

1 tablespoon anchovy paste

¹/₂ cup (4 oz / 125 g) low-fat cottage cheese

¹/₃ cup (3 fl oz / 90 ml) non-fat yogurt

2 tablespoons whole-egg mayonnaise (can use reduced-calorie mayonnaise)

2 cloves garlic, minced

2 ripe avocados, peeled and pitted

2 tablespoons lemon juice

𝓕inished 𝓠uantity
2 cups (16 fl oz / 500 ml)

1 PROCESS ALL INGREDIENTS Combine all of the ingredients in a food processor until smooth. The mixture will be fairly thin.

2 FILL JAR Spoon into a sterilized jar (see page 18).

3 SEAL Seal or cover the jar and label, if desired.

4 REFRIGERATE Refrigerate for 1 hour to thicken, or chill in the refrigerator for up to 2 days.

CAESAR SALAD DRESSING

The egg in this recipe makes a flavorsome complement to spring romaine (Cos) lettuce.

Equipment

food processor
storage jar
label

Ingredients

1 large egg, hard-cooked, shelled, and chopped

2 cloves garlic

6 tablespoons olive oil

2 tablespoons anchovy paste

1 tablespoon Worcestershire sauce

1/2 teaspoon mustard powder

1/4 cup (2 fl oz / 60 ml) lemon juice

2 tablespoons freshly grated Parmesan cheese

Finished Quantity
3/4 cup (6 fl oz / 185 ml)

1 **PROCESS EGG, GARLIC, AND OIL** Blend the egg, garlic, and oil in a food processor.

2 **ADD REMAINING INGREDIENTS EXCEPT CHEESE** Add the anchovy paste, Worcestershire sauce, mustard powder, and lemon juice. Blend well.

3 **ADD PARMESAN CHEESE** Add the Parmesan and process again.

4 **POUR INTO STORAGE CONTAINER** Pour over salad greens if using immediately, or transfer to a storage container, label if desired, and refrigerate for up to 2 days.

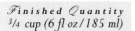

SHALLOT DRESSING

Calorie counting dieters will love this, but so will everyone else as well. The fresh taste of this dressing means that you will hardly miss the oil. It is delicious simply poured over a green salad.

Equipment

stainless steel saucepan
large mixing bowl
ice cubes
storage jar
label

Ingredients

²/₃ cup (6 fl oz / 185 ml) water

1 teaspoon arrowroot

1 tablespoon Dijon mustard

¹/₃ cup (1³/₄ oz / 50 g) finely chopped shallots

¹/₄ cup (2 fl oz / 60 ml) sherry vinegar

Finished Quantity
1 cup (8 fl oz / 250 ml)

1 COMBINE WATER AND ARROWROOT
Combine the water and arrowroot in a saucepan. Bring to a gentle boil, stirring constantly. Remove from the heat when a gravy-like consistency is reached, about 1–2 minutes.

2 CHILL AND THEN ADD REMAINING INGREDIENTS
Place the saucepan into a mixing bowl that is one-fourth filled with ice cubes and water. Allow to reach room temperature. Mix the remaining ingredients into the arrowroot mixture.

3 POUR INTO JAR AND CHILL Pour into a sterilized jar (see page 18), cover, label if desired, and chill for up to 24 hours. This dressing will keep for 3–4 days in the refrigerator.

FRESH BELL PEPPER DRESSING

The addition of bell peppers (capsicum) to this dressing is a novel change for the usual green salad. For an entirely different flavor, substitute 2 tablespoons capers for the olives.

Equipment

mixing bowl
storage jar
label

Ingredients

2 medium tomatoes, a little on the green side, chopped and drained of juice

1 cup (8 fl oz / 250 ml) whole-egg mayonnaise (low-calorie mayonnaise can be substituted)

1 tablespoon green bell pepper (capsicum), finely chopped

1 tablespoon red bell pepper (capsicum), finely chopped

1/4 teaspoon paprika

2 tablespoons chopped olives stuffed with pimento

Finished Quantity
2 cups (16 fl oz / 500 ml)

1 **COMBINE INGREDIENTS** Place all of the ingredients in a bowl and mix well.

2 **FILL JAR AND SEAL** Spoon the mixture into a sterilized jar (see page 18) and seal. Label the jar if desired.

3 **REFRIGERATE** Stored in the refrigerator, this dressing will keep for 3–4 days.

LIME CILANTRO PASTE WITH SALSA

Prepare this for the freezer when cilantro (fresh coriander) is plentiful. Combine with chopped tomatoes for a quick piquant salsa for Mexican corn chips or spread on toasted pita bread as a low-calorie appetizer.

Equipment

food processor
spatula
ice cube trays
freezer container
label

Ingredients

6 cloves garlic

2 jalapeño chilies about 2 inches (5 cm) long, seeded

1 cup (1 oz / 30 g) cilantro (fresh coriander) leaves, washed and dried

2 tablespoons fresh lime juice

2–3 medium tomatoes, seeded, drained, and chopped

pinch of salt

2 tablespoons olive oil

Finished Quantity
1 1/4 cups (10 fl oz / 315 ml)

1 PROCESS GARLIC, CHILIES, CILANTRO, AND LIME JUICE
Combine the garlic, chilies, cilantro, and lime juice in a food processor.

2 PLACE IN ICE CUBE TRAYS Using a spatula, place the mixture in ice cube trays. Freeze until needed. The frozen paste cubes will keep for several months. Once frozen, you can transfer them to a separate freezer container and label, if desired, then return to the freezer.

3 THAW AND ADD TOMATOES
Just before using, remove from ice trays, or container, and thaw. When thawed, place in a mixing bowl and add the tomatoes, salt, and olive oil.

4 MIX AND SERVE Mix until well combined and serve immediately.

CILANTRO PESTO WITH NUTS

Serve this pesto over fresh pasta or try it with Chinese rice noodles for a delicious vegetarian meal.

Equipment

food processor
storage jar
label

Ingredients

1/4 cup (2 oz/60 g) butter

3 tablespoons unsalted roasted groundnuts (peanuts)

1/2 cup (1/2 oz/15 g) loosely packed cilantro (fresh coriander) leaves

1/2 jalapeño chili, chopped

3/4 cup (6 fl oz/185 ml) groundnut (peanut) oil

1/4 cup (1 oz/30 g) freshly grated Parmesan cheese

salt to taste

Finished Quantity
1 cup (8 fl oz/250 ml)

1 PURÉE BUTTER AND NUTS; ADD CILANTRO AND CHILI Purée the butter and groundnuts in a food processor. Add the cilantro and chili and process again.

2 SLOWLY ADD OIL AND THEN CHEESE Drizzle in the oil a drop at a time. Add the Parmesan and process again. Season with salt and process again.

3 TRANSFER TO DISH Transfer to a dish or storage jar and label, if desired.

4 TO USE Pour over pasta or noodles. This recipe will only keep for 1 or 2 days in the refrigerator.

LATIN AMERICAN DRESSING WITH SALAD

This is a long-time favorite of all my family.

Equipment

mixing bowl
whisk
serving bowl
serving spoon

Ingredients

1 clove garlic, finely chopped

2 tablespoons grated onion

2 tablespoons drained capers

1 tablespoon chopped parsley

1 teaspoon chopped chives

$1/2$ teaspoon sugar

2 tablespoons herb vinegar

1 teaspoon salt

$1/2$ teaspoon pepper

$1/2$ cup (4 fl oz/125 ml) olive oil

1 avocado

2 heads romaine (Cos) lettuce, washed, dried, and torn

4–6 tomatoes, sliced

Finished Quantity
1 cup (8 fl oz/250 ml)

1 **COMBINE FIRST NINE INGREDIENTS** Combine the garlic, onion, capers, parsley, chives, sugar, vinegar, salt, and pepper in a mixing bowl.

2 **WHISK IN OIL** Whisk in the oil very slowly, a few drops at a time. The dressing will be quite thin. The dressing may be stored in the refrigerator for 3–4 days if it is not to be used immediately.

3 **ADD AVOCADO** Just before serving, peel and cube the avocado and add to the dressing.

4 ADD DRESSING TO LETTUCE

Place lettuce in a serving bowl and spoon over the dressing. Toss well to coat.

5 GARNISH AND SERVE

Garnish with the tomato slices and serve. This salad will serve 6.

ORANGE GINGER DIP

This is wonderful when used as a dip for fresh fruit, especially strawberries, or served with peaches and vanilla ice cream or mascarpone.

Equipment

mixing bowl
mixing spoon
label

Ingredients

8 oz (250 g) cream cheese, softened

1 tablespoon sugar

1 tablespoon orange zest (rind)

2 teaspoons finely chopped fresh ginger

1 teaspoon ground ginger

6–8 tablespoons fresh orange juice

pinch salt

Finished Quantity
1 cup (8 fl oz / 250 ml)

1 MIX INGREDIENTS

Combine all of the ingredients in a bowl. Stir the mixture until smooth.

2 REFRIGERATE

Cover and label, if desired. Place in the refrigerator until required. This dip will keep for 3–4 days.

DILL DRESSING WITH SMOKED TROUT SALAD

A light luncheon favorite, this dressing is as easy to make as it is delicious to eat.

Equipment

stainless steel saucepan
whisk
storage container
large serving bowl

Ingredients

¾ cup (6 fl oz / 185 ml) olive oil

1 teaspoon dried dill

3 tablespoons champagne vinegar

salt to taste

pepper to taste

12 small potatoes, boiled until tender and kept warm

1 small red (Spanish) onion, diced

1 lb (500 g) smoked trout, boned and skinned, cut into pieces

2 bunches watercress, washed and dried

Finished Quantity
1 cup (8 fl oz / 250 ml)

1 **WARM OIL; ADD DILL, VINEGAR, SALT, AND PEPPER** Warm the oil in a saucepan and, crushing the dill between your fingertips, add it to the warm oil. Add the vinegar, salt, and pepper, and whisk together. The dressing can be transferred to a storage container and refrigerated if not being used immediately. It will keep for up to 1 week in the refrigerator. Bring to room temperature before combining with the warm potato mixture.

2 **COMBINE POTATOES, ONION, TROUT, AND WATERCRESS** Combine the potatoes, onion, trout, and watercress in a large serving bowl.

3 **ADD DRESSING** Pour the dressing over the salad. Stir to mix, breaking up the warm potatoes so that they absorb all of the dressing.

4 **SERVE** Serve the salad immediately. The salad will serve 6 as a light lunch.

MALAYSIAN SATAY DIPPING SAUCE

Surround this sauce with piping hot skewers of chicken.

Equipment

mortar and pestle
wok or skillet (frying pan)
mixing spoon
serving dish

Ingredients

2 onions, chopped

2 tablespoons cayenne pepper

3 cloves garlic, chopped

1½ teaspoons grated ginger

3 chilies, chopped

1 teaspoon each coriander powder, cumin, turmeric

¼ cup (2 fl oz/60 ml) oil

2 teaspoons tamarind paste, mixed with 1½ tablespoons warm water

¼ cup (2 oz/60 g) sugar

½ cup (4 fl oz/125 ml) coconut milk

1½ cups (7 oz/220 g) ground roasted groundnuts (peanuts)

Finished Quantity
2½ cups (20 fl oz/630 ml)

1 PROCESS SPICES TO MAKE PASTE Using a mortar and pestle, make a smooth spice paste of the onions, cayenne pepper, garlic, ginger, chilies, coriander, cumin, and turmeric.

2 HEAT OIL AND ADD PASTE Heat the oil in a wok or skillet, add the spice paste, and stir-fry for about 5 minutes.

3 ADD REMAINING INGREDIENTS Add the tamarind water, sugar, coconut milk, and groundnuts. Cook for 2–3 minutes.

4 SPOON INTO DISH OR STORE Spoon into a serving dish or refrigerate for 2–3 days.

MEDITERRANEAN DRESSING WITH SALAD

Serve with bread for a complete meal that is perfect at the end of a hot summer's day.

ℰquipment

small mixing bowl
storage jar
large serving bowl

ℐngredients

3 tablespoons olive oil

1 clove garlic, crushed

¹/₄ cup (2 fl oz/60 ml) lemon juice

1 tablespoon wine vinegar

¹/₂ green bell pepper (capsicum), chopped

1 onion, chopped

¹/₂ cup (2 oz/60 g) pitted and chopped kalamata olives

¹/₄ teaspoon pepper

7 oz (220 g) canned tuna

1 lb (500 g) canned white cannellini beans

3 cups (9 oz/280 g) cooked white rice

ℱinished ℚuantity
1¹/₂ cups (12 fl oz/375 ml)

1 COMBINE DRESSING INGREDIENTS Mix together the first eight ingredients in a mixing bowl to make the dressing. If not for immediate use, transfer to a sterilized jar (see page 18), and keep in the refrigerator for up to 3 days.

2 COMBINE SALAD INGREDIENTS AND POUR DRESSING OVER Place the tuna, beans, and rice in a large bowl. Pour the dressing over the top of this mixture.

3 CHILL Chill in the refrigerator for several hours before serving. This salad will serve 4–6.

PREPARATION TIP

For variety, in place of green bell pepper (capsicum), you can use yellow, orange, or red bell peppers. Remember to remove the pith and seeds before using.

Lu Lu Paste

An old friend's mother named this spread in honor of her Aunt Lu, and as a child it was often included in summer picnics.

Equipment

medium mixing bowl
storage jar

Ingredients

1 lb (500 g) sharp cheddar cheese, grated

2 oz (60 g) black olives, pitted and sliced

7 oz (220 g) roasted red bell peppers (capsicum)

1 small onion, chopped

1/4 cup (2 fl oz/60 ml) Worcestershire sauce

1 teaspoon mustard powder

1/4 teaspoon cayenne pepper

1/4 cup (2 fl oz/60 ml) tomato ketchup

1 clove garlic, crushed

2 tablespoons fresh parsley, chopped

2–4 tablespoons whole-egg mayonnaise

Finished Quantity
3 cups (24 fl oz/750 ml)

1 **COMBINE INGREDIENTS EXCEPT MAYONNAISE** Combine all of the ingredients except the mayonnaise in a sterilized mixing bowl (see page 18).

2 **ADD MAYONNAISE AND BIND** Stir in enough mayonnaise to make the mixture bind together.

3 **REFRIGERATE** Refrigerate for 24 hours before serving to allow the flavors to combine. This paste will keep for 3–4 days in the refrigerator and is delicious spread on crackers or bread.

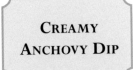

CREAMY ANCHOVY DIP

This dip is best chilled then served with fresh crudités.

Equipment

food processor
storage bowl

Ingredients

2 hard-cooked eggs

3 tablespoons Dijon mustard

1 clove garlic

2 green (spring) onions, chopped

1 large lemon, juiced

1/2 teaspoon black pepper

2 oz (60 g) anchovy paste

1 cup (8 fl oz / 250 ml) olive oil

2 tablespoons drained capers

Finished Quantity
1 1/2 cups (12 fl oz / 375 ml)

1 **PROCESS FIRST SEVEN INGREDIENTS** Combine all of the ingredients (except the oil and capers) in a food processor and process until creamy.

2 **GRADUALLY ADD OIL** Gradually add the oil, a few drops at a time, while continuing to process.

3 **TRANSFER TO A STORAGE JAR THEN ADD CAPERS** Transfer to a sterilized storage bowl (see page 18) and fold in the capers.

4 **STORE** Cover, then store this dip for 2–3 days in the refrigerator.

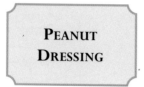

PEANUT DRESSING

Serve this over warm or cold Chinese noodles.

ℰquipment

food processor
serving bowl
storage jar

Ingredients

1 cup (1 oz / 30 g) chopped cilantro (fresh coriander)

¹/4 cup (¹/4 oz / 7 g) fresh mint

juice of 2 limes

2 cloves garlic

2 oz (60 g) fresh ginger, peeled

3 tablespoons toasted sesame seeds

4 tablespoons dry sherry

5 tablespoons soy sauce

2 jalapeño chilies, seeded and chopped

1 cup (8 oz / 250 g) chunky peanut butter

³/4 cup (6 fl oz / 185 ml) groundnut (peanut) oil

Finished Quantity
2 cups (16 fl oz / 500 ml)

1 **PROCESS FIRST FIVE INGREDIENTS** Proces the cilantro, mint, lime juice, garlic, and ginger in a food processor.

2 **ADD NEXT FIVE INGREDIENTS** Add the sesame seeds, sherry, soy sauce, chilies, and peanut butter, then process.

3 **ADD OIL** Add the oil, a few drops at a time, until it is blended into the mixture. Transfer to a serving bowl. If not using immediately, transfer to a sterilized jar (see page 18), and store in the refrigerator for up to 4 days.

4 **ADD TO FOOD AND SERVE** Combine with cooked noodles, or perhaps stir-fried vegetables, and serve immediately.

DIPS AND DRESSINGS

TAHINI DRESSING

Make an unusual salad using this dressing, or include it in a stir-fry meal.

Equipment

mixing bowl
storage jar
label

Ingredients

4 teaspoons Dijon mustard

4 teaspoons tahini (sesame paste)

1/2 teaspoon black pepper

3 tablespoons low-sodium soy sauce

4 teaspoons fresh lemon juice

1 1/2 teaspoons sesame oil

8 tablespoons red wine vinegar

4 tablespoons olive oil

4 cloves garlic, crushed

Finished Quantity
1 cup (8 fl oz / 250 ml)

1 **MAKE PASTE** In a bowl, form a smooth paste with the mustard, tahini, and black pepper.

2 **ADD REMAINING INGREDIENTS** Gradually add the other ingredients and stir until the mixture is smooth.

3 **POUR INTO JAR** Pour into a sterilized jar (see page 18), label if desired, and refrigerate. This dressing will keep for up to a week in the refrigerator.

PREPARATION TIP

Crush peeled garlic cloves with the flat of a knife to extract all of the pungent essence. Always use the freshest, plumpest garlic to insure the sharpest flavor for your dressing.

HERB AND FRUIT VINEGARS

*V*inegars, sweet or pungent, add flavor to whatever you're cooking without a single drop of added fat or sugar. Used on fruits, salad greens, fresh tomatoes and cucumbers, or as a meat marinade, herb- or spice-flavored vinegars do their job well. Flavored vinegars are attractive to look at, easy to prepare, and make wonderful gifts for your family and friends.

Gather attractive jars and bottles throughout the year. Try recycled soy sauce, vinegar, or clear wine bottles, insuring that they are completely clean, or purchase new, attractive bottles at import houses or health food stores. If ingredients continue to impart their flavors to the vinegar long after bottling and become overly intense, as is the case with garlic, you may want to steep your mixture in a wide-mouthed jar, removing the garlic after the steeping period, then transferring the vinegar to a narrow-necked bottle.

Always start with clean equipment, dish towels, hands, and work surfaces. Choose herbs that are clean, dry, and free from dark spots or bruises. Flavored vinegars infuse best in indirect light. After infusion, be sure to store in a cool, dark place and your vinegar will be at its best for up to 6 months.

SAGE AND LEMON VINEGAR

This is an especially pretty mixture and, if prepared in advance, can make a beautiful Christmas gift.

ℰquipment

*storage bottle
funnel
label*

ℐngredients

4 small sprigs fresh sage, thoroughly cleaned and dried

2 long thin spirals lemon zest (rind)

4 teaspoons white peppercorns

1 quart (1 l) white wine vinegar

ℱinished ℚuantity
1 quart (1 l)

1 **PLACE SAGE, ZEST, AND SPICES INTO BOTTLE** Place the sage, lemon zest, and peppercorns into a sterilized bottle (see page 18).

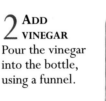

2 **ADD VINEGAR** Pour the vinegar into the bottle, using a funnel.

3 **SEAL AND STORE** Seal, label, and store for 1 month in a cool, dark place before using. The vinegar will keep for up to 6 months.

PREPARATION TIP

A lemon spiral is easiest to make by peeling one lemon continuously. Then use a knife to cut the spiral in half lengthwise, making two thinner long spirals.

PERFECT HERBED VINEGAR

Perfect herbed vinegar is easy to achieve with this no-fail step-by-step method.

Equipment

storage bottle
funnel
coffee filter paper
label

Ingredients

2 sprigs fresh sage, thyme, rosemary, or other pungent herb

2 long spirals lemon zest (rind)

4 teaspoons white peppercorns

1 quart (1 l) white wine vinegar

Finished Quantity
1 quart (1 l)

1 PLACE DRY INGREDIENTS IN BOTTLE Place the herb of your choice, lemon zest, and peppercorns in a sterilized bottle (see page 18).

2 ADD WINE VINEGAR Add the white wine vinegar, with a funnel if necessary. (You may divide this recipe into 2 bottles of 2 cups [16 fl oz/500 ml] each, halving the ingredients between each bottle.)

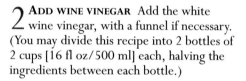

PREPARATION TIP

You can choose to heat the vinegar first and then add the herbs. This speeds up the process of steeping, but the herbs will not stay as intact if heated. When cooled, strain the mixture through coffee filter paper and bottle and label as above.

78

3 PLACE IN SUNNY WINDOW

Place in a sunny window for 2 weeks. After 2 weeks, the vinegar is ready for use.

4 FILTER IF NECESSARY

You may choose to filter the mixture for long-term use or for crystal-clear, eye-appealing gifts. Pour the mixture through several coffee filter papers, discarding the herbs, peppercorns, and lemon zest spirals.

5 REBOTTLE Rebottle, adding a new sprig or two of the herb of your choice, but omitting the peppercorns, which can darken the mixture over time.

6 STORE Label and store in a cool, dark place for up to 6 months.

PROVENÇAL VINEGAR

This vinegar is wonderful when used in a vinaigrette dressing for green salad or with a dash of olive oil as a marinade for fresh summer vegetables. Insure the herbs are washed and thoroughly dried before use.

Equipment

storage bottle
label

Ingredients

1 small sprig fresh thyme

1 small sprig fresh rosemary

1 small bay leaf

1 large clove garlic, peeled

1- x 4-inch (2.5- x 10-cm) strip lemon zest (rind)

2 cups (16 fl oz / 500 ml) white wine vinegar

Finished Quantity
2 cups (16 fl oz / 500 ml)

1 **ADD DRY INGREDIENTS TO BOTTLE** Combine the herbs, garlic, and lemon zest in a sterilized bottle (see page 18).

2 **ADD VINEGAR** Pour in the vinegar to completely cover the lemon zest and herbs.

3 **SEAL AND STORE** Seal, label, and store in a cool, dark place for about 1 month before using. This vinegar will keep for about 2–3 months stored in a cool, dark place.

This is another lovely gift idea. Keep some for yourself to use as an unusual dressing for coleslaw or salad greens.

Equipment

*double boiler
ladle
storage jar
funnel
coffee filter paper
storage bottle
label*

Ingredients

1¼ cups (10 fl oz / 315 ml) white rice vinegar

3 tablespoons honey

1½ cups (7 oz / 220 g) cranberries

1 **HEAT INGREDIENTS IN DOUBLE BOILER** In the top of a double boiler, heat all of the ingredients over simmering water for 10 minutes.

2 **LADLE INTO JAR, COVER, AND STORE** Ladle into a sterilized jar (see page 18). Cover and store for 3 weeks in a cool place.

3 **STRAIN AND REBOTTLE** Strain and funnel through coffee filter paper, pressing out all the fruit juices, into a sterilized bottle (see page 18).

4 **SEAL AND STORE** Seal and label the bottle. The vinegar is ready to use immediately. It will keep stored in a cool, dark place for 2–3 months.

SEASONAL TIP

Remember to prepare this vinegar during cranberry season to make the most of the abundant fresh berries.

*Finished Quantity
1 quart (1 l)*

This refreshing summer drink should be served over crushed ice. You can also pour it over fruit salad or brush it on barbecued fruits or poultry.

Equipment

stainless steel mixing bowl
strainer
stainless steel saucepan
ladle
funnel
storage bottles
labels

Ingredients

8 cups (2 lb/1 kg) ripe berries, such as raspberries, strawberries, blackberries, or blueberries

4 cups (2 lb/1 kg) sugar

1 quart (1 l) cider vinegar

Finished Quantity
3 quarts (3 l)

1 COMBINE INGREDIENTS Crush and combine the berries with 1 cup (8 oz/250 g) of the sugar. Pour in the vinegar. Set aside in a cool place for about 48 hours.

2 STRAIN Press the berries through a strainer, reserving the liquid and discarding the pulp.

3 TRANSFER TO PAN WITH REMAINING SUGAR, BOIL, THEN SIMMER Transfer the liquid to a saucepan and add the remaining 3 cups (1½ lb/750 g) of sugar. Bring to a boil, reduce heat, and simmer for 5–8 minutes. Skim off any foam.

4 LADLE INTO BOTTLES, LET COOL, AND SEAL Ladle into sterilized bottles (see page 18). Let cool, seal, and label if desired. Use immediately, or store in the refrigerator for 2–3 months.

LEMON GARLIC MINT VINEGAR

This is a delicious marinade for fish or poultry, and can also be used in seafood salad dressings or on green salads.

Equipment

storage bottle
label

Ingredients

4 sprigs fresh mint

3 large cloves garlic

1¹/₄-inch (3-cm) wide spiral lemon zest (rind)

1 quart (1 l) white wine vinegar

1 PLACE INGREDIENTS IN BOTTLE Place all three solid ingredients in a sterilized bottle (see page 18).

2 ADD VINEGAR Add the vinegar to completely cover the rest of the ingredients.

3 SEAL, BOTTLE, AND STAND Cap bottle, label, and let stand in a warm, bright area for about 10 days (but not in direct sunlight) before using. This vinegar will keep for about 2–3 months stored in a cool, dark place.

PRODUCE TIP

If harvesting mint from your own garden, pick the leaves just before use, to insure that they don't turn black.

Finished Quantity
1 quart (1 l)

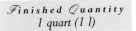

RASPBERRY VINEGAR

This vinegar makes a mild and delicate salad dressing when combined with olive oil.

Equipment

stainless steel double boiler
ladle
wide-mouthed storage jar
coffee filter paper
funnel
2 storage bottles
labels

Ingredients

3 cups (12 oz / 375 g) fresh red raspberries, lightly crushed

5 tablespoons honey

1 quart (1 l) red wine vinegar

Finished Quantity
2 quarts (2 l)

1 COMBINE INGREDIENTS IN DOUBLE BOILER
Combine all of the ingredients in the top of a double boiler and set over boiling water. Turn down the heat and simmer for about 10 minutes.

2 LADLE INTO JAR, SEAL, AND STORE Ladle into a clean wide-mouthed jar. Seal and store for 3 weeks to allow the flavors to infuse.

3 STRAIN AND FUNNEL Strain through coffee filter paper placed in a funnel directly into sterilized bottles (see page 18). Press down hard on the fruit to extract as much juice and pulp as possible. Discard all solid remains.

4 SEAL AND STORE Seal the bottles, label, and store until needed.

HERBED OILS AND INFUSIONS

The olive oils of southern France and northern Italy are as varied and distinct in taste as their wines, and almost as renowned. However, there are now also high-quality olive oils being pressed in Greece, Spain, southern California, and even parts of Australia. Walnut, almond, and hazelnut oils can also be used to add their own distinctive, delicate flavor to salads and dressings. For an Oriental taste, you may want to experiment with sesame oil.

Tasting oils is like sampling wines. For a clear, true sample, dip a piece of white bread into the oil and taste. Let your personal preference be your guide. Extra-virgin olive oil (made from the first pressing of the olives) has a low acidity and is the highest quality olive oil. For salads and dressings, buy oils labeled "cold-pressed" as these have a far greater quality of flavor. Generally, good-quality oil will keep unopened in a cool, dark place for about 2 years, but once opened, again being kept in a cool, dark place, it should be used within 6 months. Herbed and spiced oil infusions are ideal for basting broiled (grilled) meats, in salad dressings, as a simple pasta sauce, for stir-frying vegetables, or added to soups.

This is a good marinade for broiled (grilled) fish and poultry. Add 1 part vinegar to 3 parts olive oil for a green salad dressing. Insure the herbs are washed and completely dry before use.

Equipment

storage bottle
label

Ingredients

6 whole black peppercorns

3 cloves garlic, crushed

6 sprigs fresh rosemary

3 bay leaves

2 sprigs fresh thyme

2 sprigs fresh oregano

1 quart (1 l) extra-virgin olive oil

PREPARATION TIP

If fresh rosemary, thyme, and oregano are not available, experiment with other herbs, such as tarragon or lemon thyme, for different flavors.

Finished Quantity
1 quart (1 l)

1 PLACE HERBS IN JAR Place the peppercorns, garlic, and herbs in a sterilized 1-quart (1-l) bottle (see page 18).

2 ADD OLIVE OIL Add the olive oil, insuring that all the herbs are completely covered.

3 SEAL AND STORE Seal, label, and store in the refrigerator for 10 days to infuse. This oil should be refrigerated throughout all stages of the process, and will keep for up to 1 month.

HERBED OIL INFUSION

Beautiful to look at and easy to make, herb-flavored infusions are part of a culinary tradition that is still valued today. The warmth of summer can be preserved through its herbs and will bring a bright spot to winter meals.

Equipment

storage jar
clean dish towels
ladle
funnel
cheesecloth (muslin)
storage bottle
label

Ingredients

1 cup (1 oz / 30 g) fresh
basil or other herb leaves

1 clove garlic

1 cup (8 fl oz / 250 ml)
extra-virgin olive oil

1 sprig fresh basil, or other
herb for decoration

Finished Quantity
1 cup (8 fl oz / 250 ml)

1 **STERILIZE JAR** Fill the jar
with boiling water and leave
for 10 minutes. Pour out the
water and turn the jar upside
down on a clean dish towel.
Dry thoroughly.

2 **WASH AND DRY BASIL**
Meticulously
wash and dry
the basil gently
with another
clean dish
towel.

3 **PACK BASIL INTO JAR AND ADD
GARLIC** Pack the basil
tightly into the clean
jar and add the garlic.

4 COVER WITH OLIVE OIL

Cover the basil leaves with the olive oil.

PREPARATION TIPS

❧ *Always start with clean equipment, dish towels, hands, and work surfaces.*
❧ *Choose freshly picked, unblemished herbs.*
❧ *Insure that herbs are well washed and dried.*

5 SEAL AND STORE

Seal and store in the refrigerator for 2–3 weeks. Taste after 2 weeks to check intensity of flavor.

7 ADD FRESH BASIL

A fresh, clean, dry sprig of basil can be added for appearance.

6 STRAIN AND POUR INTO BOTTLE

Strain into a sterilized bottle (see step 1 for how to sterilize), through a funnel lined with cheesecloth; discard the leaves and garlic.

8 SEAL AND STORE

Seal, label, and store. This oil should be refrigerated throughout all stages of the process, and will keep for up to 1 month.

STORAGE TIP

Marinated basil leaves can be used as a substitute for fresh basil in many recipes. The flavor of the leaves lasts well, especially in the wintertime. You can save the marinated leaves frozen in ice cube trays for up to a month before using.

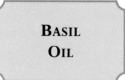

BASIL OIL

An Italian family taught me how to make "fresh" basil available all winter long. The oil can be placed in a decorative jar for special gift giving. Use the leaves, several at a time, for a "fresher" taste than dried, or pour off the oil and use to sauté tomatoes, add to a pasta dish, or stir-fry shrimp (prawns) or scallops.

Equipment

saucepan
strainer
clean dish towel
storage jar
label

Ingredients

2 cups (2 oz/60 g) fresh, clean basil leaves

about 1 cup (8 fl oz/250 ml) good quality olive oil, to fill jar

1 clove garlic, optional

Finished Quantity
2 cups (16 fl oz/500 ml)

1 BLANCH BASIL Plunge the basil leaves, in a strainer, into boiling water for 1½ minutes. Remove immediately and run cold water over the leaves.

2 PLACE ON DISH TOWEL AND DRY Turn the leaves out onto a dish towel and pat completely dry.

3 PACK LEAVES INTO JAR AND POUR IN OIL Pack the blanched leaves into a sterilized jar (see page 18) and pour the oil over the leaves. If desired, add the garlic.

4 LET STEEP Allow the flavors to steep for at least 24 hours then label and store in the refrigerator. This oil should be refrigerated throughout all stages of production, and will keep for up to 1 month.

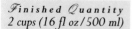

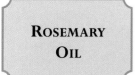

ROSEMARY OIL

Rosemary oil has been used since biblical times to soothe and heal sun-parched skin. It is also delicious rubbed on lamb before broiling (grilling) or barbecuing.

Equipment

paper towels
storage jar
funnel
coffee filter paper
storage bottle
label

Ingredients

5 tablespoons fresh rosemary leaves

2 cups (16 fl oz / 500 ml) good quality olive oil

Finished Quantity
2 cups (16 fl oz / 500 ml)

1 DRY ROSEMARY Let the rosemary leaves dry on paper towels for a few days in a warm place.

2 PLACE ROSEMARY AND OIL IN JAR, SEAL, AND STORE When the rosemary is dry, add to a sterilized jar (see page 18) and fill with the oil. Seal the jar and leave in the refrigerator for 2 weeks.

3 STRAIN INTO BOTTLE Strain the oil through the coffee filter paper placed in a funnel, into a bottle.

4 SEAL AND STORE Seal, label, and store. This oil should be refrigerated throughout all stages of the process, and will keep for up to 1 month.

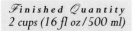

CHINESE STIR-FRY OIL

With this piquant oil in your cupboard, you can be an instant Chinese cook for any emergency meal. All you need are chopped fresh vegetables of your choice and steamed rice.

Equipment

heavy-based skillet
(frying pan)
cleaver / sharp knife
chopping board
funnel
coffee filter paper
storage bottle
label

Ingredients

2 cups (16 fl oz / 500 ml) groundnut (peanut) oil

8 slices fresh ginger

5 cloves garlic

5–6 green (spring) onions, trimmed of roots and 2 inches (5 cm) of green tops

Finished Quantity
2 cups (16 fl oz / 500 ml)

1 HEAT OIL Heat the oil slowly in a heavy skillet.

2 ADD GINGER, GARLIC, AND GREEN ONIONS Crush the ginger and garlic with the wide blade of a cleaver or knife and add to the warm oil. Add the green onions. Heat slowly for 8 minutes, or until the onions become translucent.

3 LET COOL AND STRAIN INTO JAR Let the oil cool and then strain through coffee filter paper placed in a funnel, into a sterilized storage bottle (see page 18).

4 SEAL AND STORE Seal the jar, label, and store. The oil should be refrigerated throughout all stages of the process, and will keep for up to 1 month. The oil may become cloudy, but will return to a clear state when warm.

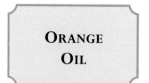

ORANGE OIL

Orange oil is especially good for sautéeing fresh carrots or sprinkling over a platter of fried rice and vegetables just before serving.

Equipment

storage jar
cheesecloth (muslin)
funnel
bottle
label

Ingredients

$1/2$ teaspoon coriander seeds

2 cloves garlic

3 slices fresh ginger

5 whole cloves

24 whole allspice berries

zest (rind) of 1 orange

1 small cinnamon stick

good quality olive oil,
to fill the jar

Finished Quantity
2 cups (16 fl oz / 500 ml)

1 ADD SPICES AND OIL TO JAR Fill a sterilized jar (see page 18) with all of the spices and the oil.

2 STORE Store in the refrigerator for at least 2 weeks to allow the spices to infuse.

3 STRAIN Strain out the spices through a funnel lined with cheesecloth, directly into a storage bottle.

4 SEAL AND STORE Seal and label, if desired. The oil should be refrigerated throughout all stages of the process, and will keep for up to 1 month.

SERVING TIP
This orange-flavored oil can also be used to baste turkey, chicken, or duck, or as a delicious fruity salad dressing.

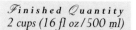

MAIL ORDER SOURCES

Altrusa Corporation
Ball Home Canning
Products,
Consumer Affairs Dept.
P. O. Box 2729
Muncie, IN 47307
(317) 281-5009

Compliments to the Chef
374 Merriman Ave
Ashville, NC 28801
(704) 258-0558
(800) 895-CHEF

Macy's
The Marketplace
151 West 34th Street
New York, NY 10001
(212) 695-4400
(800) 456-2297

Williams-Sonoma
Mail Order Department
P. O. Box 7456
San Francisco, CA
94120-7456
(415) 652-9007
(800) 541-2233

MAIL ORDER SEEDS AND PLANTS

The Herbfarm
32804 Issaquah/Fall City
Road, Fall City,
WA 98024

Le Jardin du Gourmet
West Danville, VT 05873

Sandy Mush Herb
Nursery
316 Surrett Cove Road
Leicester, NC 28748
(704) 683-2014

Shady Hill Gardens
803 Walnut Street
Batavia, IL 60510
(312) 879-5665

Shepherd's Garden Seeds
Shipping Office
30 Irene Street
Torrington, CT 06790
(203) 482-3638

A BIBLIOGRAPHY OF ADDITIONAL READING

Andrews, Glenn. *Making and Using Flavored Vinegars.* Pownal, VT: Garden Way Publishing, 1991, Pub. #A112

Creber, Ann. *Oils and Vinegars.* Rutland, VT: Charles E. Tuttle Co., 1992

Freid, Mimi. *Making Liqueurs for Gifts.* Pownal, VT: Garden Way Publishing, 1991, Pub. #A101

Gunst, Kathy. *Condiments.* New York: G. P. Putnam's Sons, 1984

Hopley, Claire. *Making and Using Mustards.* Pownal, VT: Garden Way Publishing, 1991, Pub. #A129

Oster, Maggie. *Herbal Vinegar.* Pownal, VT: Storey Publishing, 1994

Tolley, Emelie & Chris Mead. *The Herbal Pantry.* New York: Clarkson N. Potter, Inc., 1992

Van Garde, Shirley. *Food Preservation and Safety: Principles and Practice,* Iowa State University Press, 1994